Spotlight on
ANCIENT CIVILIZATIONS
GREECE

Ancient Greek TECHNOLOGY

Henry Bensinger

Published in 2014 by The Rosen Publishing Group, Inc.
29 East 21st Street, New York, NY 10010

First Edition

Editor: Joanne Randolph
Book Design: Kate Vlachos

Photo Credits: Cover DEA/L. Romano/De Agostini Picture Library/Getty Images; p. 4 DEA/G. Nimatallah/De Agostini Picture Library/Getty Images; pp. 5, 9 (right), 14, 17, 21 DEA/G. Dagli Orti/De Agostini Picture Library/Getty Images; p. 7 Roman/The Bridgeman Art Library/Getty Images; p. 8 Clive Streeter/Dorling Kindersley/Getty Images; p. 9 (left) Werner Forman/Universal Images Group/Getty Images; p. 10 © iStockphoto.com/Mlenny Photography; p. 11 (left) Kamira/Shutterstock.com; p. 11 (right) Panos Karas/Shutterstock.com; p. 12 Rechitan Sorin/Shutterstock.com; p. 13 Dorling Kindersley/Getty Images; p. 16 DEA Picture Library/De Agostini Picture Library/Getty Images; p. 18 © iStockphoto/Maria Toutoudaki; p. 19 Neveshkin Nikolay/Shutterstock.com; p. 20 DEA/A. Dagli Orti/De Agostini/Getty Images; p. 22 Apic/Hulton Archive/Getty Images.

Library of Congress Cataloging-in-Publication Data

Bensinger, Henry.
Ancient Greek technology / by Henry Bensinger. — First edition.
    pages cm. — (Spotlight on ancient civilizations: Greece)
Includes index.
ISBN 978-1-4777-0774-6 (library binding) — ISBN 978-1-4777-0881-1 (pbk.) —
ISBN 978-1-4777-0882-8 (6-pack)
1. Technology—Greece—History—To 146 B.C.—Juvenile literature. 2. Greece—
Civilization—To 146 B.C.—Juvenile literature. I. Title.
T16.B46 2014
509.38—dc23

                                                              2013002100

Manufactured in the United States of America

CPSIA Compliance Information: Batch #S13PK2: For further information contact Rosen Publishing, New York, New York at 1-800-237-9932

CONTENTS

Ancient Greek Technology

Ancient Greek craftsmen, such as pottery makers, developed technology to make their jobs easier to do.

Think about all the tools we use each day that make life easier. People use **technology** to make doing different jobs easier. You likely cannot imagine life without cars or televisions. At one point, though, these things did not exist. The building blocks for many modern inventions got their start in ancient Greece thousands of years ago.

The Greeks invented the first water wheels, water mills, clocks, three-masted ships, canal locks, and so much more. An ancient Greek man even invented the first vending machine.

Greeks had the technology to dig up, melt, and shape metal. The metal was used to make many useful and beautiful objects.

Tools for Agriculture

Greece has rocky, poor soil. Despite this fact, people have used the land for farming since ancient times. The earliest Greek farmers likely used simple tools, such as sticks, to help them dig. Over time, though, better technology was invented. Oxen pulled wooden plows to break up the soil and prepare it for planting.

Greece also does not get much rain. Once again, the ancient Greeks were able to come up with technology to solve this problem. They created **irrigation** systems that brought water in from rivers and streams to their fields.

This ancient Greek mosaic shows a man using an ax to cut grape vines. Grapes were one of the main food crops grown in ancient Greece.

Indoor Plumbing

Just as the ancient Greeks were able to pull water to their fields, they were also able to bring it into their homes. **Archaeologists** have found bathtubs and toilets that flushed, just as ours do today.

The Greek scientist Archimedes is believed to have invented the water screw. This tool pulled water from its source to pipes that could carry the water elsewhere.

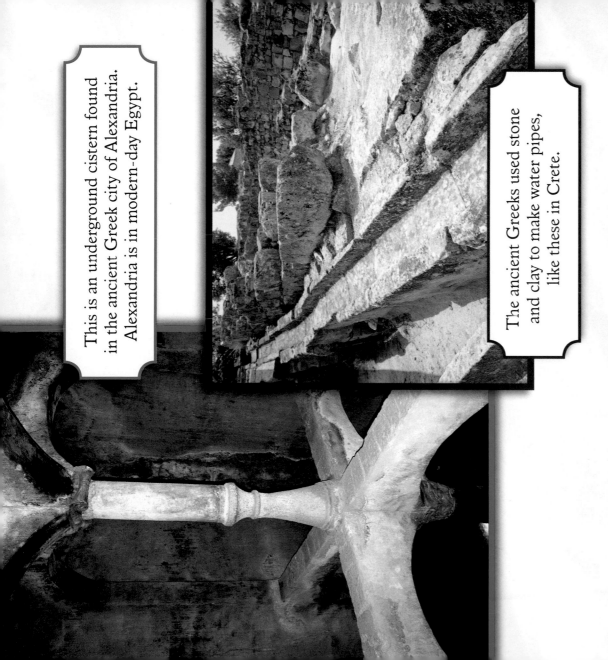

This is an underground cistern found in the ancient Greek city of Alexandria. Alexandria is in modern-day Egypt.

The ancient Greeks used stone and clay to make water pipes, like these in Crete.

The Greeks used clay or stone pipes to carry the water. They used **aqueducts** to carry water from rivers and streams to **cisterns** in the town. Fountains were connected to the cisterns. People could draw fresh drinking water from them as needed.

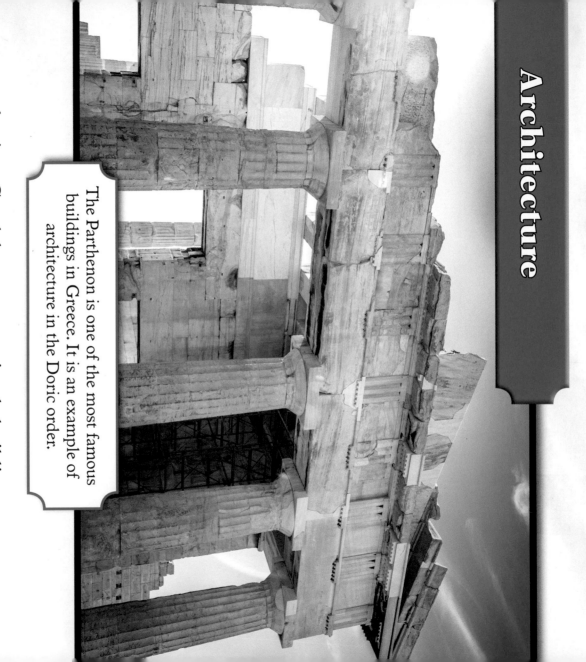

The Parthenon is one of the most famous buildings in Greece. It is an example of architecture in the Doric order.

Ancient Greek homes were simple buildings made of sun-dried mud bricks. They generally had a courtyard at their center and rooms surrounding it. The homes were designed to stay cool in the summer and warm in the winter.

Greek temples were very different from Greek houses. They were large stone buildings with many columns. The two most common styles, or orders, of **architecture** were the Doric and Ionic orders. The easiest way to tell these orders apart is by looking at the columns. Doric columns were very plain. Ionic columns had a scroll-like design at the top.

Here you can see the scroll designs at the top of this Ionic column.

There was a much fancier style of column, too. Buildings with these columns were in the Corinthian order, but it was not as common as the other two.

Construction Methods

The ancient Greeks needed technology to build their temples. Special tools were needed to cut rocks from a **quarry**. Slaves generally did this job. Stonemasons then chiseled, or chipped, the rocks into the needed shapes.

Here you can see that columns were not a long, single piece. They were large blocks stacked on top of one another. You can see the columns rest on a base of large square blocks, too.

This modern-day image shows how the stone workers of ancient Greece likely shaped the stone they used in building. They had chisels and hammers very similar to these.

These rocks were often very large. To move them to the building site, they were put on sleds or rollers. **A winch** was used to help men lift the heavy blocks. The ancient Greeks used wooden structures called **scaffolding** to let workers climb to where the stones needed to go.

Greece is a **peninsula** and a group of islands in the Mediterranean Sea. It is no surprise that the ancient Greeks created technology to let them better use the resources of the sea. They built small ships with sails to carry goods to other places to trade. They also made large but light warships, called triremes. These ships had sails but they also had many oars that men on the ship used to row. Both kinds of ships were fitted with heavy metal anchors to keep the ships from floating away when not moving.

Fishermen used stone and metal tools to catch and clean fish. They also made nets from animal and plant **fibers.**

This fresco shows Greek triremes coming into a port. A fresco is a painting made on stone.

Weapons

Greece's rocky ground has many metal deposits. The Greeks used this metal to make many useful objects, including weapons and armor. Most Greek weapons were made from iron because it was the most

This painting shows a Greek soldier with a shield, spear, and armor. The armor and weapons Greek soldiers wore and carried were quite heavy.

plentiful metal. Metal was heated in a fire or furnace until it began to melt. When it was soft enough, it was hammered into the needed shape.

Most Greek soldiers fought using spears, which had a metal tip on a long wooden handle. They carried a shield made from metal or animal hides. They also wore armor made from metal.

Ancient Greeks also used swords, javelins, slingshots, and the bow and arrow against their enemies. This ancient Greek sword with its gold handle and bronze blade was probably used for decoration only.

This piece of marble shows a Greek doctor checking a patient.

For a while, if a person in ancient Greece got sick, he or she would pray to the god of healing, named Aesclepius, for a cure. Luckily a man named Hippocrates offered another solution. He believed that if a person was sick it was because the body was

Hippocrates is perhaps best known for creating the Hippocratic oath, which is still used by doctors today. The oath outlines some rules doctors must follow to keep patients safe.

not working properly. He did not think people got sick because they had made the gods unhappy.

Several ancient Greeks who lived after Hippocrates continued the study of medicine and the human body. Herophilus studied **anatomy**. Erasistratus, another Greek man, was interested in studying how the blood moved through the body.

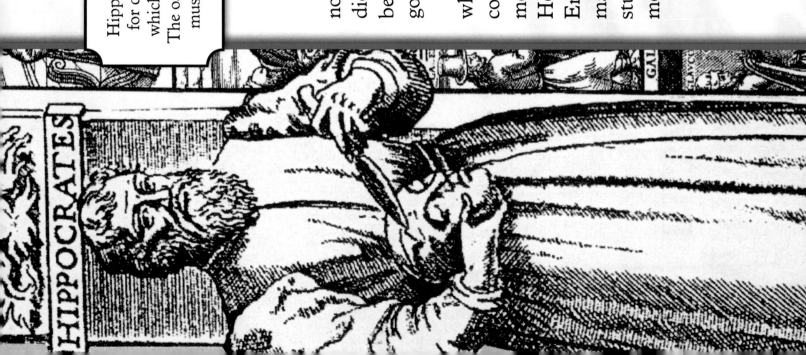

HIPPOCRATES

Tools for Surgery

Scientists are not sure who did the first surgery in history. They do believe that Hippocrates performed surgeries in the 400s BC, though. He used a scalpel to cut into a person's body. Scalpels are sharp metal tools.

This carving shows some surgical instruments used in ancient Greece.

Here a Greek surgeon uses a scalpel to cut a patient's arm and let a small amount of blood escape. Bloodletting was a common treatment for illnesses in ancient Greece.

Ancient Greek doctors also used hooks. Some hooks were used to gently move things, such as veins, so doctors could see them better. They were also used so doctors could hold back the edges of a wound. There were no medicines to keep patients from hurting, but Greek doctors did their best to make sick people well again.

Paving the Way

Many ancient Greek ideas and inventions have served as the building blocks for our modern way of life. The technology started in ancient Greece was used and improved by the societies that came after them. The ideas of Greek mathematicians, such as Euclid and Pythagoras, are still studied today. Aristarchus was the first to figure out the length of the year. The technology the Greeks used improved their lives. It also paved the way for better lives for all of us today, too.

The lighthouse in Alexandria, Egypt, was the tallest building on Earth for hundreds of years. This lighthouse, built by Greek architect Sostratus, was one of the seven wonders of the ancient world.

GLOSSARY

anatomy (uh-NA-tuh-mee) The study of the body.

aqueducts (A-kweh-dukts) Channels or pipes used to carry water for long distances.

archaeologists (ahr-kee-AH-luh-jists) People who study the remains of peoples from the past to understand how they lived.

architecture (AR-kih-tek-cher) The art of creating and making buildings.

cisterns (SIS-ternz) Tanks for storing water.

fibers (FY-berz) Thread or threadlike parts.

irrigation (ih-rih-GAY-shun) The carrying of water to land through ditches or pipes.

peninsula (peh-NIN-suh-luh) An area of land surrounded by water on three sides.

quarry (KWOR-ee) An area of land where stones for building can be found.

scaffolding (SKA-fohld-ing) A stand raised above the ground for workers and materials.

technology (tek-NAH-luh-jee) The way that people do something using tools and the tools that they use.

winch (WINCH) A machine that has a roller on which a rope is wound for pulling or lifting.

INDEX

WEBSITES

Due to the changing nature of Internet links, PowerKids Press has developed an online list of websites related to the subject of this book. This site is updated regularly. Please use this link to access the list:
www.powerkidslinks.com/sacg/tech/